AF269522

# VENEZUELA

BY CYNTHIA KENNEDY HENZEL

Essential Library

An Imprint of Abdo Publishing
abdobooks.com

Printed in the United States of America, North Mankato, Minnesota.
102022
012023

Cover Photos: Shutterstock Images (Canaima National Park, pattern)
Interior Photos: Alejandro Solo/Shutterstock Images, 4–5; Shutterstock Images, 7, 8, 10, 25, 34–35, 40–41, 60, 97, 101; Vadim Petrakov/Shutterstock Images, 13; Sergi Reboredo/VW Pics/AP Images, 14–15; Ricardo Ribas/SOPA Images/Light Rocket/Getty Images, 16; Peter Hermes Furian/Shutterstock Images, 18 (Venezuela); Web Tools/Shutterstock Images, 18 (globe); Maria Averburg/Shutterstock Images, 19; Jonas Piontek/Novarc Images/Mauritius Images GmbH/Alamy, 22–23; Stanislav Duben/Shutterstock Images, 26–27; Nature Photo/Shutterstock Images, 29; Jan Woitas/Picture Alliance/dpa/AP Images, 30–31; Joshua Stevens/EOSDIS LANCE/NASA, 33; Reyes Photo/Shutterstock Images, 37; Pesek Photo/Shutterstock Images, 38; Jimmy Villalta/VW Pics/AP Images, 43, 54–55; Oxford Science Archive/Print Collector/Hulton Archive/Getty Images, 45; Archivart/Alamy, 47; Dea/M. Seemuller/De Agostini/Getty Images, 48; Heritage Images/Hulton Fine Art Collection/Getty Images, 50; AFP/Getty Images, 51; Juan Manuel Hernandez Husband/Anadolu Agency/Getty Images, 58; Rjankovsky/Alamy, 61; Jesus Vargas/Picture Alliance/dpa/AP Images, 63; Featureflash Photo Agency/Shutterstock Images, 64; Bertrand Parres/AFP/Getty Images, 66–67; Getty Images News/Getty Images, 71; Edilzon Gamez/Getty Images News/Getty Images, 72; Rodrigo Abd/AP Images, 75, 84; Meridith Kohut/Bloomberg/Getty Images, 76; Federico Parra/AFP/Getty Images, 79, 80–81, 95; Yuri Cortez/AFP/Getty Images, 83; Jhonny Parra/AFP/Getty Images, 86; Irena Misevic/Shutterstock Images, 88; Rodrigo Buendia/AFP/Getty Images, 90–91; Joe Raedle/Getty Images News/Getty Images, 93; Matias Delacroix/AP Images, 99

Editor: Angela Lim
Series Designer: Maggie Villaume

Library of Congress Control Number: 2022940387

**PUBLISHER'S CATALOGING-IN-PUBLICATION DATA**
Names: Henzel, Cynthia Kennedy, author.
Title: Venezuela / by Cynthia Kennedy Henzel
Description: Minneapolis, Minnesota: Abdo Publishing, 2023 | Series: Essential Library of Countries | Includes online resources and index.
Identifiers: ISBN 9781532199516 (lib. bdg.) | ISBN 9781098274719 (ebook)
Subjects: LCSH: Venezuela--Juvenile literature. | South America--Juvenile literature. | Venezuela--History--Juvenile literature. | Geography--Juvenile literature.
Classification: DDC 987--dc23

# CONTENTS

# A TOUR OF VENEZUELA

Abby and her parents were planning their big summer vacation. The family loved to travel, and they talked about all the places they had been. Everyone agreed that one of their best vacations had been their trip to Venezuela. In a single week they had seen the capital city of Caracas, gone scuba diving, and visited some of the most beautiful natural areas on Earth.

On that trip, the family arrived at Simón Bolívar International Airport. The hotel sent a car, so they loaded their luggage and rode toward the city. Their hotel was right on the coast. The sand was pure white, and the ocean was a lovely turquoise color.

The capital city of Caracas is located at the foot of the
coastal extension of the Cordillera de Mérida mountains.

The water was the perfect temperature for swimming. The country is just north of the equator, so temperatures in Venezuela are consistent throughout the year.

The next morning, Abby and her parents had a big breakfast of *perico venezolano*, a Venezuelan dish of scrambled eggs with tomatoes, onions, coriander, and ground peppers. The dish is named for its bright colors. *Perico* is Spanish for "parrot." The perico venezolano was served with avocados and arepas, which are flattened, fried corn breads. Abby dipped the arepas in a warm chocolate sauce. The chocolate sauce was mixed with melted cheese, giving it a savory taste. The sauce with the arepas was a delicious combination.

After breakfast, Abby and her parents took a taxi to Plaza Bolívar in central Caracas. The plaza dates back to 1567. There, they saw a giant bronze statue of Simón Bolívar on a horse standing in the middle of the plaza. Bolívar was born in Caracas in 1783. He led the independence movement in Venezuela and five other South American countries, helping liberate these countries from Spain. Bolívar is nicknamed the Liberator for his role in Venezuelan independence. It didn't take long for Abby to realize that lots of places and buildings in the country were named after Bolívar.

Abby saw many important government buildings, such as City Hall and the building that houses the National Assembly, located around the plaza. Her family enjoyed seeing the Metropolitan Cathedral of Saint Anne, more commonly known as the Caracas Cathedral, on the east side of the plaza. Abby and her parents visited this Roman Catholic cathedral. While there, they learned it was first built in the 1600s, but it had been destroyed by an earthquake in 1641. It was rebuilt between 1665 and 1713. Abby's mother thought the cathedral, with its rounded arches

The statue of Simón Bolívar in Plaza Bolívar was made in Munich, Germany, and unveiled in Venezuela in 1874.

and beautiful artwork, was lovely. The cathedral includes several chapels along the sides. Simón Bolívar's parents and wife are buried in one of the side chapels. A statue of the Liberator is also located in the chapel.

Caracas has other iconic buildings, such as the Municipal Theater of Caracas and the Archbishop's Palace. One of Abby's favorite buildings was the National Pantheon, where many of the country's heroes and historic figures—including Simón Bolívar—are buried. The National Pantheon was originally built as a church, but it became a burial spot in 1874. The marble interior has large murals illustrating famous battles from the Venezuelan War of Independence (1810–1823). The main part of the building has a monument to the Liberator that contains Bolívar's bronze coffin.

For lunch, the family decided to try Venezuela's national dish, *pabellón criollo*. It consisted of a plate of shredded beef, black beans, and white rice served with fried plantains. Plantains are in the banana family, but they are less sweet than most bananas eaten in the United States. They are starchy and are typically served cooked rather than eaten raw. Abby's parents enjoyed an espresso. The coffee beans used in the espresso were grown in the northwestern part of Venezuela. The country is also famous for the chocolate it produces. So, following their filling meal, Abby and her parents took a trip

## CACAO

Venezuela's geography and climate are ideal for growing cacao. Each year, the country produces approximately 22,000 short tons (20,000 metric tons) of cacao, the basic ingredient in chocolate.[1] At the end of the 1700s, it was the world's biggest producer of cacao. But dictators have seized many of the country's cacao plantations and limited their exports. Today, Venezuela produces less than 1 percent of the world's cacao.[2] Still, Venezuelan cacao is a highly coveted ingredient for high-end chocolate makers in Europe and the United States. Venezuelan cacao beans are less bitter than other cacao beans grown around the world.

to a local chocolate factory, where they sampled chocolates made from Venezuelan cacao beans.

Later that afternoon, they went to Maripérez Station and rode the *teleférico*, the cable car system, to El Ávila National Park. The 2.1-mile (3.4 km) ride to the park took about 15 minutes.[3] The view was spectacular! From the summit of Mount Ávila, Abby could see the beautiful Caribbean Sea and the sprawling city of Caracas. The park was crowded. Many people from Caracas visited the park to hike and enjoy other outdoor activities while taking in the scenic views.

## VENEZUELA'S COASTS

The next part of their vacation was a two-day diving trip off the northern coast of Venezuela. Abby and her parents traveled to the Los Roques archipelago. The chain of islands became a national park in 1972. The park is known for its well-preserved coral reefs. Venezuela has more than 300 islands and cays, and there are diving sites at many of them.[4] The family took a small airplane out to Gran Roque, the main island of the archipelago. They went to the dive shop to get outfitted with scuba equipment. Then they climbed onto a boat for a guided tour of the diving site.

Los Roques National Park protects the Caribbean coast and its wildlife.

The archipelago has two large coral barrier reefs. These reefs are important because they protect the shoreline. The coral serves as a natural barrier against strong waves and tsunamis. As the boat glided over the blue waters, Abby and her parents faced a decision. There were a lot of things to see underwater. Divers could explore underwater caves or shipwrecks that dated to the 1500s. The family went to an area with a wall of soft coral and strands of coral called sea whips. The wall extended more than 197 feet (60 m) underwater.[6] As Abby and her parents slowly submerged, thousands of fish darted about. It was a magical world of brightly colored coral, anemones, fish, and other sea creatures. Their guide led them along the colorful coral wall. Abby thought she glimpsed a large fish called a barracuda swimming by.

After two days of sand and surf, Abby and her parents caught another plane to the southeastern part of Venezuela to see Canaima National Park, a United Nations Educational, Scientific and Cultural Organization (UNESCO) World Heritage site. The park has 11,563 square miles (29,947 sq km) of pristine rain forest and huge vertical rock cliffs.[7] Table mountains called *tepuis* make up 65 percent of the park.[8] Angel Falls, the world's tallest waterfall, is located in Canaima National Park.

It was a difficult journey to the falls. Many tourists chose to see the magnificent waterfall from an airplane, but Abby's family canoed and hiked through the rain forest. Abby's dad saw a jaguar slinking through the trees. Her mom enjoyed the many birds, such as dusky parrots and macaws, but she shrieked when a green-and-black poison dart frog dropped from a low branch into the canoe. It was a long hike, but Angel Falls was worth the hard work. The family stood in awe, watching the water cascade from the top of a tepui and tumble thousands of feet below.

Angel Falls drops from a height of 3,212 feet (979 m).[9]

As Abby and her parents shared memories of their trip, they recalled that their time in Venezuela had been exhausting. In only one week, the family had been swimming, diving, canoeing, and hiking. They had explored historic buildings in the capital city and visited a rain forest. As the family continued planning its next vacation, they hoped it would be as exciting as the one they had taken to Venezuela.

## ABOUT VENEZUELA

Venezuela is a diverse country with landscapes including rain forests, beaches, and savannas. In the northwest, there are even arid sand dunes. Venezuela has 43 national parks, which cover more than 20 percent of the country.[10]

Venezuela is also an oil-rich country. It has been one of the leading producers of oil since the early 1900s. Though the oil can generate great wealth for the nation, it has also contributed to the country's instability. Venezuela's economy improves when worldwide oil prices are high, but it crashes when the oil industry suffers. Today, approximately 90 percent of the country's exports are fossil fuels.[11]

### POISON FROGS

Many of the brightly colored frogs in South and Central America have toxins stored in their skin. They use the toxins for defense, and their bright colors warn predators that the frogs are poisonous. However, these poisonous frogs do not produce poison themselves. Recent studies have shown that these toxins develop because of the frogs' diets. These frogs have adapted to eat ants and other insects that produce toxins. The frogs can then store and concentrate the toxins from the insects. When these kinds of frogs are raised in captivity, they lack toxins.

Political turmoil has added to the country's economic problems. President Nicolás Maduro came to power in 2013. Since then, he has been accused of being a dictator and failing to protect the people of Venezuela. Because of the instability and high crime rates in the country, the US government issued travel restrictions and strong recommendations that US citizens should not go to Venezuela. A trip like the one Abby's family took would be difficult today because of these restrictions.

Venezuela has some of the best-preserved landscapes and most beautiful beaches in Latin America. It has abundant biodiversity in regions that have been relatively unexplored by modern scientists. In addition, the mix of European, Black, and Indigenous people living in the country contribute to Venezuela's unique culture.

Angel Falls plunges from the Auyán Tepuí, which means "Devil's Mountain" in the Pemón Indigenous language.

# CHAPTER TWO

# GEOGRAPHY

Venezuela has an area of 352,144 square miles (912,050 sq km), which is about half the size of Mexico.[1] Venezuela is in the northern part of South America. The Caribbean Sea and Atlantic Ocean form the country's northern border. Guyana lies to the east, and Brazil lies to the south. Colombia is to the west of Venezuela.

The country has a tropical climate due to its proximity to the equator. There is also little seasonal change in temperature. However, regions may have varying weather patterns because of differences in elevation. For example, mountainous regions tend to have cooler temperatures than the lowlands. Most of the country has an average temperature higher than 75 degrees Fahrenheit (24°C).[2]

Lush forests grow along central Venezuela's Orinoco River.

Sandboarders walk along the dunes of Médanos de Coro National Park, one of the areas of Venezuela where rainfall is rare.

Weather patterns in Venezuela can be divided into the wet season and the dry season. The wet season lasts from May through November. Landslides may occur during the wet season as a result of heavy rains. These natural disasters cause extreme damage to houses and other buildings.

The dry season goes from December until April. Elevation affects how much water an area receives. The high mountains in the northwestern part of the country create a rain shadow effect. It is difficult for moisture to travel over the mountains that separate Colombia and Venezuela. As a result, the region of Venezuela directly east of these mountains is arid in comparison with other regions in the country.



Venezuela is subject to frequent earthquakes. The country sits on the boundary between two tectonic plates, which are large sheets of land that make up Earth's crust. Tectonic plates move and slide against each other, causing earthquakes. Caracas and other major cities lie on this boundary. They could experience significant damage if a major earthquake struck the region.

Earthquakes have devastated Caracas in the past. An earthquake in 1812 destroyed much of the city and killed approximately 20,000 people.[3] In 2021, geologists studied the region and found severe strain along the tectonic plates, suggesting that a powerful earthquake could strike in the future.

Venezuela can be divided into four geographic regions. The Venezuelan Highlands lie in the northwestern part of the country and include two mountain ranges. The Maracaibo Lowlands are also in the northwest and are situated between the mountain ranges. Los Llanos, also called the Orinoco Plains, are in central Venezuela. The Guiana Highlands are the largest geographic region in

# VENEZUELA

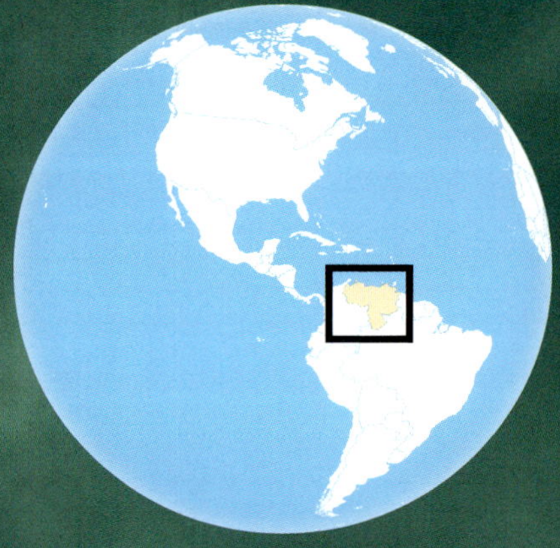

**KEY:**
- Capital
- City
- Point of Interest

Venezuela, covering more than half of the country. The region extends through much of the southern and eastern parts of Venezuela.

In addition to mainland Venezuela, the country has more than 300 islands. Many of these islands are uninhabited, including La Tortuga Island, which has an area of about 60 square miles (155 sq km).[6] Other islands in Venezuela are popular for tourism. Margarita Island features white sand beaches and lovely views of the Caribbean Sea. Visitors can enjoy water activities such as swimming, snorkeling, and diving. In addition, the island is famous for its pearl industry.

Hurricanes and tropical storms sometimes strike Venezuelan islands and the northern coast of the country during the wet season. Hurricanes and tropical storms are similar types of extreme weather, but hurricanes have higher wind speeds than tropical storms. In Venezuela, hurricanes are rarer than tropical storms. Both can cause heavy rain, flooding, and landslides.

# VENEZUELAN HIGHLANDS

Northwestern Venezuela has two mountain ranges, the Serranía de Perijá and the Cordillera de Mérida. Both are part of the Andes Mountains system. The Serranía de Perijá runs along the border between Venezuela and Colombia. The Cordillera de Mérida mountain range lies southeast of the Serranía de Perijá.

The Cordillera de Mérida contains the highest point in Venezuela, Pico Bolívar. Smaller extensions of the Cordillera de Mérida, such as the Coastal Range and the Interior Range, run parallel to the Caribbean coastline. Caracas rests in the Coastal Range near the Caribbean Sea. The Segovia Highlands are a set of high plains and hills along the coast.

Mountains in the Serranía de Perijá and the Cordillera de Mérida are not as high as other peaks in the Andes Mountains. Because of the lower altitude, much of the Venezuelan Andes is forested. Several national parks protect these forests. However, the ecosystem is still at risk because of mining and agricultural expansion. Some of the higher peaks rise above the tree line. The Humboldt Glacier, one of the world's few tropical glaciers, lies high in the Cordillera de Mérida.



The Humboldt Glacier rests on the side of Pico Humboldt, the second-highest point in Venezuela. It is the last remaining glacier in the nation, but it is in danger of disappearing. The glacier has been shrinking at an alarming rate due to climate change. The ice is less than 65 feet (20 m) thick.[7] The glacier has an area of less than 0.018 square miles (0.046 sq km).[8] Scientists predict that the glacier will melt completely before 2040.

# MARACAIBO LOWLANDS

The Maracaibo Lowlands are between the Serranía de Perijá and the Cordillera de Mérida mountain ranges. The lowlands are home to Lake Maracaibo, which the region is named after. Some people consider Lake Maracaibo to be the largest lake in South America. Others consider it an inlet from the Caribbean Sea rather than a natural lake. The lake is connected to the Caribbean Sea by a 25-mile (40 km) channel.[9] Several freshwater rivers flow into the lake, but it also mixes with water from the Caribbean Sea during high tides. This causes water in the lake to be somewhat salty.

Lake Maracaibo is one of the oldest lakes in the world, having formed approximately 36 million years ago. Today, the Maracaibo Lowlands region is known for its oil reserves. It produces two-thirds of Venezuela's petroleum.[10] Early reports of oil discoveries date back to the 1500s, when Spanish sailors used tar oil seeping from the ground to seal leaks on their ships.

The Maracaibo Lowlands include the only desert in Venezuela. Sand dunes called Médanos are protected by Médanos de Coro National Park, which is near the city of Coro. The sand dunes can

Lake Maracaibo holds the world record for the location with the highest concentration of lightning.

reach a height of 130 feet (40 m).[12] In addition to sand dunes, the park features salt marshes. The area receives little rainfall, and the sand dunes shift constantly because of the strong winds in the region.

## LOS LLANOS

Los Llanos are an area of lowlands that extends from south of the Maracaibo Lowlands to eastern Venezuela. The main feature of Los Llanos is the Orinoco River, the country's major waterway. The river begins near Venezuela's southern border and flows in both this country and Colombia, eventually emptying into the Atlantic Ocean. *Orinoco* originates from

The Orinoco River flows for approximately 1,330 miles (2,140 km).[13]

the Indigenous language Warao and means "a place to paddle." Before roadways and air service were available in the country, the Orinoco River was the main way to travel to the central part of Venezuela.

Mountains cast rain shadows in some portions of the Orinoco Basin, and these regions receive little rainfall. Other areas of Los Llanos receive heavy rainfall, which supports the growth of rain forests. Like most of Venezuela, rainfall varies depending on the time of year. During the dry season, the savannas of Los Llanos can be arid and dusty. But rivers in the region may flood during the rainy season. Temperatures are fairly consistent year-round throughout Los Llanos.

## GUIANA HIGHLANDS

The Guiana Highlands are found in southern and eastern Venezuela, along the country's borders with Colombia, Brazil, and Guyana. These highlands lie south of Los Llanos and are the most remote parts of Venezuela. The region is known for its steep tepuis, which are part of the Pacaraima Mountains. The tepuis are capped with hard rock and are resistant to erosion. The rocks found in the Guiana Highlands are some of the oldest on Earth, with some estimates dating the rocks to two billion years ago.

The Guiana Highlands are known for their stunning geography. High tepuis have sheer cliff faces. Rain is common year-round. The heavy rainfall in the region gives rise to lush forests and beautiful waterfalls. The Amazon Rain Forest extends into this region, providing habitats for many plants and animals. The Guiana Highlands also have many minerals, including iron and diamonds. Mount Roraima is one of the most famous tepuis in Venezuela. It is located near Venezuela's borders with Guyana and Brazil. Standing 9,094 feet (2,772 m) tall, Mount Roraima is the tallest tepui in the Pacaraima Mountains.[14] Auyán Tepuí is another famous tepui in the Guiana Highlands. Home to Angel Falls, it is one of the most iconic sites in Venezuela.

Geologists estimate that tepuis such as Mount Roraima formed two billion years ago.

Venezuela is a tropical country close to the equator. It has a variety of landscapes, including coastal islands and rocky tepuis. Areas at low altitudes are covered with deserts or rolling plains. Ample rainfall allows wildlife to thrive, and Venezuela is home to many species of plants and animals.

# CHAPTER THREE

# PLANTS AND ANIMALS

**V**enezuela is one of the most diverse countries in the world in terms of plant and animal life. It is home to approximately 21,000 plant species.[1] More than 4,000 animal species live in the country.[2] Scientists consider Venezuela a megadiverse country, one of 17 in the world. A megadiverse country has at least 5,000 endemic, or native, plant species and a marine system within its borders. Together, the megadiverse countries account for 70 percent of the world's plant and animal life.[3]

Different regions of Venezuela support different types of plants and animals. Elevation plays a factor in the wildlife of a certain region. Savannas and forests are the most common landscapes in the country.

The blue-and-yellow macaw is one of more than 1,380 known bird species in Venezuela.

The Caribbean Sea is full of wildlife, making Venezuela a popular snorkeling and diving destination. Coral reefs are home to many types of fish, including butterfly fish, angelfish, and nurse sharks. The Caribbean Sea is also the habitat of many endangered species. Hawksbill sea turtles and bottlenose dolphins are just two examples of marine life that have experienced population loss since the early 2000s. Though the turtles are protected by Venezuelan law, hunters illegally kill them for their beautiful shells and as a source of meat. Oil spills and pollution affect marine life too.

Venezuela's national bird, the troupial, can be seen on Caribbean islands. Troupials are large birds with orange bodies, growing to be about nine inches (23 cm) in length.[4] They have black heads and tails, and their wings are black with a white stripe. Troupials are nicknamed bugle birds because of their songs.

A strip of mangrove forest runs along the northern coast of Venezuela. Smaller mangrove forests are found on some islands in the Caribbean. Crocodiles, crab-eating raccoons, and crab-eating foxes live in mangrove forests. Large rodents, such as the spotted paca, also call these forests home.

**There are approximately 8,000 native plant species in Venezuela.[5]**

## VENEZUELAN HIGHLANDS

Much of the country's northern mountain region is tropical and forested. Pino de pasto and

Hawksbill sea turtles spend much of their lives in coral reefs, but they can also be found in the open ocean. These turtles are critically endangered.

Mexican alders are common trees in the region. Trees do not grow at high elevations above 10,170 feet (3,100 m).[6] Vegetation transitions into grasslands and scrublands at this altitude. This type of ecosystem is called páramo and is found only at high elevations in parts of the Andes.

Common plants include tussock grasses and giant rosette plants. Giant rosette plants are leafy with thick stalks. They do not typically grow taller than 33 feet (10 m).[7] Plants at high altitudes tend to be shorter than plants at lower elevations, which helps them withstand cold temperatures.

Though unforested, the páramo ecosystem of the Cordillera de Mérida is extremely biodiverse. Animals such as foxes, weasels, and guinea pigs live in the grasslands. The area provides habitat for poison dart frogs and rocket frogs. Endangered animals such as the spectacled bear and mountain tapir also live at these elevations. Tapirs are black with white bodies. They look similar to pigs but are more closely related to horses. They have short trunks that they use to grab food such as fruits and leaves.

The Serranía de Perijá mountains that straddle Venezuela and Colombia are home to rare birds. Some are found only in these mountains, such as the Perijá metaltail, a type of hummingbird. Other birds, such as the golden-headed quetzal and Andean condor, are also found in these mountains. The Serranía de Perijá are not well explored, and scientists believe that there are still bird species in this region that have not yet been discovered.

Young tapirs have spots and stripes that help them blend in with their surroundings.

# MARACAIBO LOWLANDS

The Maracaibo Lowlands include dry forests and savannas. The nanche plant is one of the shrubs found in this region. It grows to about 33 feet (10 m) tall and produces yellow fruit that can be used to make desserts and drinks.[8] Bark from the nanche plant can be used to treat leather, making the leather more durable. It is also used in traditional medicinal practices, as the bark has antimicrobial properties. Mangrove forests are found near Lake Maracaibo. Other plants include the threadleaf beakseed and the dagger cactus.

The grasslands of the Maracaibo Lowlands are habitat to a number of rodents, including the Guajira mouse opossum and the Hummelinck's vesper mouse. These creatures, as well as other animals living in the lowlands, have adapted to the dry habitat. Small birds, including the chestnut piculet and various hummingbird species, flit about this region. Lake Maracaibo provides habitat to the Guiana dolphin and the greater flamingo.

Pollution, deforestation, and hunting threaten animals in the lake and surrounding areas. The Maracaibo Basin is known for its oil resources, and human activity in the region has reduced the amount of forested land in the lowlands. Oil pipelines run underneath Lake Maracaibo, but many of these pipelines are in need of repair. Constant leaks have polluted the lake and harmed wildlife. Agricultural runoff also contaminates the lake with pesticides and fertilizers. Oil spills and pesticides have resulted in algae blooms that lower oxygen levels, making it difficult for animals and plants to survive in the waters. The pollution in Lake Maracaibo is so severe that the oil spills and algae blooms can be seen from space.

Algae blooms cause Lake Maracaibo to appear green in color on a satellite image.

The environmental crisis in the Maracaibo Lowlands is worsened by economic problems in Venezuela. Prices have soared in the country, which has made food unaffordable for many Venezuelan citizens. Though many animals are protected under Venezuelan law, some people have resorted to killing wildlife in order to feed themselves.

# LOS LLANOS

Los Llanos include savannas and wetlands that are home to many plant and animal species. Swamp grasses are common, and carpet grasses grow in drier areas of Los Llanos. The region does not have many trees, but scrub oak does grow in this part of Venezuela.

The rich wildlife of Los Llanos attracts tourists who come to see anteaters, armadillos, howler monkeys, and deer. Capybaras, the largest rodent species in the world, live in Los Llanos. The region is also home to several species of wild cats, including jaguars, cougars, and ocelots.

Caimans, which are related to alligators, float along the Orinoco River. Piranhas, giant otters, and freshwater dolphins also swim through this waterway. The Orinoco River is also home to more than 300 species of fish, including electric eels.[9] The green anaconda, one of the largest snake species in the world, lives in the Orinoco Basin. Female anacondas are much larger than males. These snakes are olive with dark spots. Their coloration provides camouflage as they hunt underwater, lying in wait for large animals such

> **Green anacondas can grow to be 29 feet (8.8 m) long and weigh up to 550 pounds (249 kg).[10]**

Green anacondas can find prey by sensing vibrations through the ground.

as capybaras, deer, and tapirs. Green anacondas are a type of boa constrictor. They wrap around and squeeze their prey before swallowing the meal whole.

The plants and animals found in Los Llanos can be markedly different between the wet and dry seasons. The region is often flooded during the wet season, and animals adapted to a wetter climate can be found in Los Llanos during that time. During the dry season, much of the wetlands evaporate, leaving behind a few watering holes. Wetland animals concentrate in the watering holes, which also attract birds and other creatures.

Humans have contributed to habitat loss in Los Llanos. The savannas are used as pastures for cattle. Other areas of Los Llanos are cleared for growing crops such as rice and corn.

## GUIANA HIGHLANDS

Lichen, grasses, and orchids are common across the tepuis of the Guiana Highlands. This region also has carnivorous plants, such as pitcher plants. These plants are named for their pitcher-like shape. They can grow at high altitudes and in rocky areas. Their pitchers secrete nectar to attract insects and small animals, but the pitchers are filled with water. The creatures fall into the pitcher and drown when they try to drink the nectar. Small hairs along the opening of the pitcher make it difficult for creatures to escape.

Rain forests cover portions of the Guiana Highlands. They are home to a wide range of animals. Seven species of cats live there, including jaguars, ocelots, cougars, margays, and jaguarundis. Jaguarundis are long, slender cats. Their colors vary depending on where they live. They are darker in rain forests and reddish in dry, open areas. Birds such as dusky parrots, harpy eagles, red-shouldered macaws, and toucans live in the rain forests of Venezuela.

Several types of primates inhabit the rain forest, including owl monkeys and capuchin monkeys. Owl monkeys are small, nocturnal monkeys. Capuchins live in groups. They are black with white chests and faces. They are named for the black caps of hair on the tops of their heads, which resemble the cowls of Capuchin monks. Capuchins are intelligent. They can use objects as tools, such as using rocks to crack nuts.

Rodents such as the fiery squirrel and the Orinoco agouti are endemic to the highlands.

## ORCHIDS

Venezuela has more than 1,000 known species of orchids.[13] The Easter orchid is the country's national flower. It grows high in the canopy of dense forests of northern Venezuela. The Easter orchid is also called the *flor de mayo*, or "flower of May," because it tends to bloom in May. The orchid varies in color. Typically pink or white, the Easter orchid can also be red or purple.

Capuchin monkeys can use their tails for balance.

Agoutis walk on their toes and look like large guinea pigs. The Guiana Highlands also provide

habitats for many reptile and amphibian species. The bushmaster is one snake species found

in the highlands. It is one of the deadliest snakes in the world, capable of striking quickly and

injecting large amounts of venom. Its bite is often fatal. The tegu lizard can grow to be four feet

(1.2 m) long and is known for its large appetite.[14] In Venezuela, the tegu is nicknamed the chicken wolf, because it sometimes breaks into chicken coops to eat eggs. The tegu also eats fruits and vegetables. Yellow-banded poison dart frogs are found in the Guiana Highlands. They are brightly colored, and their skin secretes toxins.

Political instability that began in the early 2000s has led to environmental issues in Venezuela. As the country deals with political and social challenges, wildlife conservation and environmental policies have fallen by the wayside. In 2022, the Venezuelan government had not released new environmental information on its websites since 2011. Scientists within the country have talked about the lack of governmental aid in conservation.

Venezuela remains one of the most ecologically diverse countries in the world. The country has several national parks that protect the land and its wildlife. Canaima National Park, which is located in the Guiana Highlands, is the largest in the country. These national parks have the potential to attract tourists from around the world, and Venezuela has many unique animals that are of interest to scientists.

# CHAPTER FOUR

# HISTORY

The first peoples may have arrived in the Venezuelan region as early as 13,000 BCE. Some people came overland from modern-day Brazil and the Guianas. Others arrived from the north, sailing over the Caribbean Sea.

By the 1500s CE, the Kalina, Arawak, and Muisca were among the major peoples in the Venezuela area. Each early nation in Venezuela had a distinct culture and lifestyle. The Kalina people lived near the Caribbean coast and near the Orinoco River. They were experts at sailing, navigation, and basket weaving. The Arawak settled in the tropical forests, where they farmed, hunted, and fished. They established small settlements in the region. The Muisca peoples included several nations that spoke Chibcha languages.

Many Warao people live in stilt houses along the Orinoco River today.

They lived on the slopes of the Andes, where they farmed and traded with peoples in the lowlands. The Muisca peoples built irrigation channels to water crops, which included maize and potatoes.

The Warao were another major nation in Venezuela in the 1500s. They settled in the Orinoco delta and surrounding wetlands. *Warao* means "people from the marshland." They were mainly hunters and gatherers, but they also built houses on top of stilts to keep the structures above the water. Today, more than 50,000 Warao people live in Venezuela, making them one of the largest Indigenous populations in the country.[1] Many other Indigenous nations are recognized in Venezuela today.

## SPANISH COLONIALISM

In 1498, Christopher Columbus became the first European to enter the Venezuela area. Spanish explorers in the 1500s were the ones to name the region Venezuela, meaning "little Venice." The Warao houses and surrounding waterways reminded the explorers of the Italian city famous for its canals.

At first, the Spanish did not try to establish colonies in Venezuela, but their arrival still threatened Indigenous nations in the area. They forced Indigenous people to dive for pearls and enslaved others. The Spanish had negative opinions of the Indigenous peoples in Venezuela, which they used to justify these cruelties. For example, they viewed the Kalina as fierce warriors and cannibals, likely exaggerating the customs of these people.

Architecture in Coro has Spanish influences. The town was the first capital of Venezuela.

The Spanish established the first European settlement in Venezuela in the 1520s. Called Cumaná, it was located on the Caribbean coast and became an important site for the pearl industry and for trade. The Spanish founded the city of Coro in northwestern Venezuela in 1527. Soon after its founding, the Spanish king Charles V leased Coro to Germany. Germans—along with Spaniards and other European explorers—believed there was gold to be found in South America. The Germans used Coro as a base to launch expeditions for El Dorado. Many Europeans believed this was a legendary city of gold hidden in the South American rain forests. The Spanish regained control of Coro in 1546 when the lease expired. Colonies on the Caribbean coast were vulnerable to pirate raids, so Coro was moved farther inland for protection.

Throughout the 1500s, the Spanish established more colonies in Venezuela, including Caracas in 1567. Caracas became an agricultural center, especially for wheat and cacao, and the Spanish established the encomienda system to increase production. As part of the encomienda system, Spanish officials were given tracts of land, gaining authority over the Indigenous people who lived in the area. They forced the Indigenous people to pay tribute in the form of gold, crops, or labor. The Spanish were often cruel—demanding large tributes and excessive labor from the Indigenous people—and the encomienda system functioned as a form of enslavement.

The Spanish also had a strict caste system based on race. Spaniards born in Europe were at the top of society. Creoles, people of Spanish descent who were born in South America, also had influential roles. Indigenous people, Black people, and people of mixed ancestry were lower in status. Under the caste system, the Spanish enslaved Indigenous and Black people, forcing them to work on plantations. Many of the enslaved Black people arrived in Venezuela as a result of the slave trade. Spanish and other European explorers kidnapped people from Africa and forced them into hard labor.

## VENEZUELAN INDEPENDENCE

The Spanish government established the Viceroyalty of New Granada in 1717. This viceroyalty was seated in present-day Bogotá, Colombia, and governed the surrounding region that included Venezuela. Tensions between European Spaniards and Creoles began to rise during this time. Creoles were unhappy with Spanish rule and high taxes.

Overseas, Spain was at war with France. King Ferdinand VII of Spain was held prisoner

Many enslaved people in Venezuela were forced to work on cacao plantations.

during this war, and Venezuelan Creoles saw this as an opportunity. On April 19, 1810, Venezuela declared its independence from Spain. At first the new government, known as the First Republic of Venezuela, declared only temporary independence. They would return to Spanish rule after Ferdinand VII reclaimed the throne. But radicals, including Simón Bolívar, pushed for full independence. Then on July 5, 1811, Venezuela declared full independence from Spain, becoming the first country in South America to do so.

War followed this declaration. The fight for independence was challenging, and Bolívar was exiled from the region several times. An earthquake in 1812 devastated Caracas and destabilized the First Republic of Venezuela, leading to Bolívar's first exile. The following year, he reestablished himself as a leader in the revolution and reclaimed Caracas. This became known as the Admirable Campaign. However, Spanish forces and Venezuelans supportive of Spanish rule remained in the area. They forced Bolívar into exile once again. He regained control of the Venezuelan army in 1817. In 1819, Bolívar's army was deadlocked in a battle against Spain, with neither army strong enough to finish the other off. Bolívar decided

## FRANCISCO DE MIRANDA

In 1806, Francisco de Miranda, a soldier who had fought in both the American Revolution and the French Revolution, attempted to help Venezuelans win their independence from Spain. He drove the Spanish out of Coro but held the town for only two weeks. Eventually, de Miranda was forced to sign a temporary truce with Spain. Though de Miranda was unsuccessful in leading Venezuela to independence, his efforts allowed many to believe that independence was possible.

# SIMÓN BOLÍVAR

Simón Bolívar was born in Caracas on July 24, 1783. One of his tutors, Simón Rodríguez, introduced Bolívar to the philosophical work of Jean-Jacques Rousseau. These readings influenced his thinking about ethics and government. Bolívar was also inspired by the American Revolutionary War (1775–1783).

Bolívar went to Spain for his education when he was 16 years old. While there, he married a Spanish noblewoman. He returned to Caracas with his wife, but she died of yellow fever less than a year after their marriage. After her death, Bolívar went back to Europe and studied the works of philosophers. Inspired by these writers and by the success of revolutions in the United States and France, Bolívar vowed to liberate his own country from Spain.

Bolívar succeeded in liberating Venezuela, Ecuador, Peru, Bolivia, and Colombia. He had hoped to create a single united country in South America. But fighting in the areas he liberated eventually led to the creation of multiple countries. He stepped in as dictator of these countries in 1828. He survived an assassination attempt that year. Bolívar died in 1830 while returning to Europe.

Bolívar served as the first president of Gran Colombia from 1819 to 1830.

Simón Bolívar won the Battle of Carabobo, achieving independence from Spain for the Republic of Gran Colombia.

to have his army retreat across the Andes Mountains into present-day Colombia. In doing so, he was able to recruit Colombian volunteers to join his forces.

On December 17, 1819, Bolívar formed the Republic of Gran Colombia, which included present-day Venezuela, Colombia, Ecuador, and Panama. The Battle of Carabobo was the final battle in the war for independence from Spain, and Bolívar's army emerged victorious on June 24, 1821. After liberating Gran Colombia, Bolívar worked to liberate Peru from Spain as well. During his absence, Venezuela became its own country in 1829.

# ESTABLISHING A GOVERNMENT

After becoming independent, Venezuela struggled to establish a stable government. From 1830 until 1935, various caudillos, or military leaders, came into power. José Antonio Páez, a general during the war for independence, became the first president of Venezuela in 1830. He created a constitution that centralized the government. He also set plans in motion to build Venezuela's economy. Páez was a conservative leader who often aligned with landowners and wealthy merchants. He received little opposition until 1848, when the Liberal Party that represented the working class grew in power. The Liberal Party formed in 1840. In the late 1840s, Venezuela's economy began to decline. This led to increasing opposition against Páez and his Conservative Party.

José Tadeo Monagas and his brother José Gregorio Monagas rose to power and ruled as dictators between 1848 and 1858. The Monagas brothers were originally aligned with the Conservative Party but incorporated liberal policies over time. Under their rule, Venezuela's economy worsened. The brothers attempted to instate a new constitution that would have extended their reign and eliminated term limits. Liberals and Conservatives joined together to oust the brothers. They were successful in ending the Monagas dynasty but were unable to establish political stability afterward.

The Federal War (1859–1863) erupted as Conservatives and Liberals fought for control of Venezuela. During these years, power changed hands multiple times. Páez returned to power and ruled from 1861 to 1863, but Liberals ultimately won the Federal War. They drafted a new constitution. The government remained unstable in the following years. José Tadeo Monagas briefly regained power in 1868, but the Liberals, led by General Antonio Guzmán Blanco, overthrew the Conservatives in 1870.

In 1872, Guzmán Blanco approved a new constitution. It called for suffrage for all males and democratic election of a president. Venezuela's government prospered under Guzmán Blanco, attracting foreign investors. In addition, he established standardized education and expanded the country's agricultural industry. However, Guzmán Blanco was also criticized for being a dictator. He severely limited the Roman Catholic Church and censored the Venezuelan press.

## 1900s VENEZUELA

At the beginning of the 1900s, Venezuela was once again ruled by a dictator. Cipriano Castro,

José Antonio Páez served under Bolívar and later fought for Venezuela's independence from Gran Colombia.

Venezuela's growing oil economy attracted many immigrants to the country in the mid-1900s.

a caudillo, took control of the presidency in 1899 and ruled until 1909. He was unpopular and saw multiple revolts during his time as president. Castro's military, which was led by General Juan Vicente Gómez, had to deal with these uprisings. When poor health forced Castro out of the presidency in 1909, Gómez took charge.

Under Gómez, Venezuela's economy transformed. Oil was discovered near Lake Maracaibo in 1914, and the country became the world's largest oil exporter. Gómez managed to eliminate Venezuela's foreign debt. He modernized the country, building roads and upgrading the military. Though the economy flourished, Gómez was also a harsh dictator. He censored the press and used spies to get rid of his political opponents. He used his political influence to buy farms, businesses, and other properties, becoming the wealthiest person in the country. Meanwhile, many Venezuelans lived in poverty.

Military leaders took control of the presidency following Gómez's death in 1935. But in 1945, the president was overthrown by a civilian group that consisted of members of the Democratic Action political party. The party drafted a new constitution that would help support the working class. In 1947, Rómulo Gallegos became the president. He and the Democratic Action party taxed the petroleum industry and encouraged the formation of labor unions.



Gallegos's presidency was short-lived. Conservative forces staged a coup that drove him out of office just eight months after he was elected. These forces stopped the labor movement and closed universities. The Democratic Action party regained control in 1959 and established a more moderate administration than it had in 1947. The government worked to grow the country's agricultural industry, improve health care, and eliminate illiteracy.

For nearly 40 years, Venezuela's democratic government was relatively stable and did not experience uprisings or protests from civilians. However, the country's stability became intertwined with global petroleum sales. In the 1970s, rising oil prices added to economic inequality in Venezuela, benefitting the wealthy class while people living in poverty saw little relief.

In the late 1980s, world oil prices dropped significantly. This had devastating effects in Venezuela. The country found itself deep in debt.

Carlos Andrés Pérez became president in 1989. Venezuela received a loan from the International Monetary Fund, and Pérez limited government spending in attempts to boost the economy. The government's policies were unsuccessful, and prices skyrocketed. The cost of a bus ride rose by 30 percent in 1989, and Venezuelan citizens took to the streets in protest.[4] Caracas erupted in violence, with protesters rioting in the city. The government also responded with violence, and security forces killed approximately 3,000 people.[5]

In the early 1990s, Pérez faced two unsuccessful coup attempts. Lieutenant Colonel Hugo Chávez and other army officers led the first attempt in 1992. Chávez was imprisoned for his involvement in the coup. He became an influential political figure. Many Venezuelans were frustrated with the government and saw him as someone who could reform the country. President Rafael Caldera Rodríguez released Chávez from prison and dropped the charges against him. Chávez ran for president in 1998 and won the election with 56 percent of the popular vote.[6] He remained president of Venezuela until his death in 2013. He left a complicated legacy. Some Venezuelans praise his efforts toward social reform, while others accuse him of being a dictator. His death, along with economic troubles, have contributed to the instability that Venezuela faces today.

In 1998, more than 50 percent of the Venezuelan population was living in poverty.[7]

# PEOPLE AND CULTURE

The majority of Venezuelans today identify as mestizo and have a mixed heritage that includes European, Indigenous, and African ancestries. Mestizos make up approximately 51.6 percent of the country's population. White people with exclusively European ancestry make up 43.6 percent of the population. More than 3 percent of the country is Black, and more than 2 percent is Indigenous.[1]

Because the country was a Spanish colony for hundreds of years, many Venezuelans today have Spanish ancestry. Others come from German descent. Many Europeans immigrated to Venezuela in the

Venezuelans travel to El Ávila to gather palm leaves for the Palmeros. This celebration occurs on Palm Sunday, a Roman Catholic holy day.

mid-1900s because of the country's growing petroleum industry. People arrived from Italy and Portugal. The Venezuelan government encouraged immigration during the oil boom of the 1970s as well, and many people entered from other parts of South America, including Argentina, Chile, and Uruguay. Today, most Venezuelans live in urban areas in the northern and western parts of the country. Caracas and Maracaibo are the most-populated cities.



Venezuela recognizes 44 Indigenous nations.[2] Some Indigenous people live alongside Venezuelans of different heritages. But some Indigenous nations are more isolated and practice traditional lifestyles. The Wayuu and the Warao are two of the largest nations in Venezuela, with thousands of members each. The Wayuu raise livestock and live on La Guajira Peninsula, which is known for its coal deposits. The Warao people live near the Orinoco Delta, and their lifestyles are influenced by the river. They fish, travel in canoes, and use palm leaves to build houses and hammocks. The majority of Indigenous people live in the forests surrounding Lake Maracaibo. A smaller number live in the Guiana Highlands.

Spanish is the official language of Venezuela. English is also commonly spoken in major cities. Many business workers communicate in English, and the language is often taught in private schools. In addition, approximately 25 Indigenous languages are spoken in the country.[3] Most of the languages belong to the Cariban, Arawakan, or Chibchan language groups.

# RELIGIOUS AND CULTURAL CELEBRATIONS

Approximately 96 percent of the population identifies as Roman Catholic. Protestants make up 2 percent of the population.[5] Other religious traditions, including Judaism and Islam, are also practiced in Venezuela.

As a primarily Roman Catholic country, Venezuela celebrates Carnival, a festival that has its roots in Catholicism. Traditionally, Carnival is celebrated before the season of Lent, a 40-day period characterized by prayer and fasting that is celebrated by Catholics and some other Christians.

## FREEDOM OF RELIGION

Today, the Venezuelan constitution grants the freedom of religion. Guzmán Blanco established religious freedom during his presidency in the 1870s and 1880s. His policies led to a separation of church and state and allowed civil marriages. However, Guzmán Blanco sometimes targeted Roman Catholics, taking away lands from Catholic churches and closing religious convents.

Carnival has been celebrated in Venezuela since colonial times. The largest Carnival festival in Venezuela takes place in El Callao, and festivities last for several days. Although Carnival festivals occur throughout South America, El Callao Carnival is recognized by UNESCO for its blend of cultural traditions. Influences from Afro-Caribbean cultures, such as calypso music, are present in the celebration.

The country has other Roman Catholic celebrations. The Fiesta de San Pedro and San Pablo honors Saint Peter and Saint Paul, who were two of Jesus's apostles. The festival blends Catholicism

Venezuelan dancers for the San Francisco de Yare Corpus Christi celebration are part of voluntary Christian associations. Each association makes its own devil masks.

with Indigenous traditions and includes music, storytelling, and street food. The coastal city of San Francisco de Yare celebrates the Roman Catholic holiday of Corpus Christi. Drawing from local traditions, people in Yare dress in devil costumes and dance while moving backward. Others play maracas and other instruments to ward off evil spirits. The festival symbolizes good prevailing over evil.

Venezuela also has nonreligious celebrations. New Year's Eve festivities typically begin around 8 p.m. on December 31. These celebrations involve many traditions and superstitions meant to improve luck and fortunes in the coming year. One tradition involves lentils. Some people eat them during their meals, and others hold uncooked lentils in their hands as the clock strikes midnight. They may also throw lentils in the air. The lentils are meant to increase one's chances of success in the new year.

# FOODS

Venezuelan foods have roots in Spanish, West African, and Indigenous traditions. Popular foods in Venezuela tend to feature domestically grown crops and tropical fruits. Corn is a major crop grown in the country. Arepas are a type of bread made with water, salt, and *masarepa*—a precooked ground corn flour. The mixture is flattened into a disk and cooked in oil on a grill.

Another corn-based favorite is *hallaca*, a sweetened cornmeal dough cooked in banana leaves that is often made at Christmas. Hallaca is typically seasoned with annatto seeds, giving it a mild nutty or floral flavor. Annatto also gives hallaca its dark-orange color.

Rice, beef, and black beans are staple foods in Venezuela. These are often served in a stew. Some people consider pabellón criollo—a rice dish served with black beans, steak, and tomatoes—to be Venezuela's national dish. There are many variations of pabellón criollo. The steak may be replaced by other meats such as fish, alligator, or *chigüire*, which comes from capybaras. Pabellón criollo is also sometimes served with a fried egg on top or with a side of plantains. *Tequeños* are another popular food in Venezuela. This appetizer or snack consists of feta cheese that is covered in flour and fried.

Venezuelan cuisine also includes many desserts. One favorite is tres leches, a sponge cake that is soaked in three types of milk: condensed milk, evaporated milk, and regular milk or cream. The cake is then topped with meringue. *Dulce de lechosa* is a popular papaya-based dessert. Though it is most commonly served around the Christmas holidays, it is enjoyed year-round.

## ARTS

Venezuela is home to many writers and artists. Rómulo Gallegos is a famous novelist who was born in 1884. His works often feature the natural wonders of Venezuela, such as Los Llanos and rain forests, and they also include elements of local folklore. Gallegos also served as Venezuela's president from February through November of 1948, until a military coup overthrew him.

Carlos Raúl Villanueva is the father of modern architecture in Venezuela. His most well-known designs were for the Central University of Venezuela in Caracas. His designs included the university's Olympic Stadium and the School of Architecture. He also designed the school's auditorium. The ceiling of the auditorium is made of floating panels of varying sizes that improve the acoustics of the room.

Modern Venezuelan artists include sculptor Jorge Blanco, who was born in 1945. He uses nontraditional materials for his sculptures, including synthetic fabrics, rope, and mirrors to create art that inspires joy. Paul del Rio is a painter and sculptor known for his harsh depictions of city life as well as his political cartoons.

Lía Bermúdez was a Venezuelan sculptor. She was born in Caracas in 1930 but spent much of her career in Maracaibo. Many of Bermúdez's

The *Caracas Sphere*, a sculpture by Jesús Soto, is made of 1,800 hollow orange tubes.

works can be seen throughout these two cities, including at the Supreme Tribunal of Justice in Caracas. Her abstract sculptures are often inspired by natural forms such as shells and butterflies.

Venezuela is home to many art museums. One of the most famous is the Caracas Museum of Contemporary Art, which houses works from famous artists including Salvador Dalí and Pablo Picasso. Other art installations can be seen in Caracas too. One of the most notable is the Caracas Sphere, which is located next to a highway in the city. Created by Jesús Soto, the sculpture is made of orange aluminum bars that are suspended to create a spherical shape. The installation moves in the wind and shimmers in the light.

## MUSIC

Venezuelans enjoy their own versions of Caribbean merengue and salsa. Oscar D'León is a famous Venezuelan salsa artist. In addition, the country has its own music history in joropo and llanero music. Joropo is fast-paced, rhythmic dance music. The lead instrument is a plains harp. Instruments such as maracas and a type of four-stringed guitar known as a cuatro accompany the plains harp. Joropo is also the name for the style of dance that goes along with the music. Joropo dance styles differ by region.

Llanero music is another Venezuelan genre. Some consider it to be a subgenre of joropo. Llanero music has influences from European waltzes and African music. Many llanero songs draw from the culture of Venezuelan cattle herders in Los Llanos, telling tales about the life of the cowboy.

A student in Venezuela's El Sistema music program plays her violin in the San Agustín neighborhood of Caracas.

The Venezuelan government sponsors a symphony orchestra as well as the Simón Bolívar Youth Orchestra. The country's music program began in 1975. It allows children from all social classes to learn to play an instrument and to try out for professional youth orchestras. Music can have a significant impact on a child's life and is shown to improve social, creative, and mental skills. Venezuela's music program has inspired other countries around the world to take up similar initiatives.

## SPORTS

Baseball came to Venezuela from the United States in the early 1890s. By the early 1900s, the game had grown extremely popular, with baseball teams in major cities. The country established its own professional league in 1927. The Venezuelan national team began competing in major baseball championships in 1938, appearing in the Central American and Caribbean Games. It won its first championship title in 1941, besting Cuba in the Amateur World Series.

Today, baseball is the most popular sport in Venezuela. Since 1939, nearly 400 Venezuelans have played in Major League Baseball in the United States.[6] Shortstop Luis Aparicio was born in Maracaibo and made his major league debut on April 17, 1956. That year, he won the American League Rookie of the Year Award. He led the American League in stolen bases for nine consecutive seasons, a record that remained in place in 2022. Aparicio was inducted into the Hall of Fame in 1984, becoming the first Venezuelan-born player to earn this achievement.

In 2022, Detroit Tigers slugger and Venezuela native Miguel Cabrera got his 3,000th career hit. He became the seventh player in MLB history to have 3,000 hits and 500 home runs.[7] Many sports experts believe that Cabrera will be inducted into the Hall of Fame in the future.

Traditional sports in Venezuela include *coleo*, or bull-tailing. In coleo, a bull is released into a corral and four people must chase it and bring it down in the shortest time possible. One person grabs the bull's tail to bring it down, and then the other three people help immobilize it. The sport dates back to the 1500s and is still popular today.

Another traditional sport is *bolas criollas*. Similar to bocce, players must throw balls to land as close as possible to a smaller target ball. Bolas criollas is particularly popular in the Los Llanos region and rural areas.

# CHAPTER SIX

# POLITICS

Hugo Chávez ran for president in 1998, vowing to reform the Venezuelan government and stamp out corruption. Chávez's platform included helping the poor and reducing the power of the wealthy class. During his first year as president, Chávez received an approval rating of 80 percent.[1] This widespread support allowed him to draft and pass a new constitution. The constitution increased presidential terms from five years to six. After the constitution was approved, Venezuela held new elections. Chávez was reelected to serve as president.

The new constitution established the Bolivarian Republic of Venezuela. It increased the powers of the president and transformed the government. It improved human rights, allowed free education

Hugo Chávez began his first presidential campaign on August 8, 1998.

and free health care, and acknowledged the rights of Indigenous peoples. It also combined the bicameral legislative branch into a single house.

## BRANCHES OF GOVERNMENT

The 1999 constitution established Venezuela as a federal presidential republic. It created five branches of government: the executive branch, the legislative branch, the judicial branch, the electoral branch, and the citizens' branch. The president is the head of the executive branch and is elected by popular vote. The presidential term lasts for six years. The 1999 constitution limited the president to two consecutive terms, but a 2009 amendment allowed the president to run indefinitely. The president is responsible for nominating the vice president and cabinet members. In addition, this position oversees foreign relations and declares states of emergency. Nicolás Maduro became president in 2013 following Chávez's death and was reelected in 2018. Many believe the 2018 election was rigged in Maduro's favor.

### DRAFTING A NEW CONSTITUTION

Chávez created the Constituent National Assembly (ANC) to draft the 1999 constitution. The ANC worked quickly, first convening in February 1999. The constitution was in effect by July 2000. It required all public officials to be elected, and a massive election took place. Many of the government officials who had not previously been elected were replaced. Chávez was able to restructure the National Assembly with his supporters in the 2000 elections.

The legislative branch consists of the unicameral National Assembly. The National Assembly is responsible for making laws, creating taxes, and keeping the executive and judicial branches in check. Following the 2020 election, the National Assembly was made up of 277 deputies, including three deputies who represented Indigenous nations.[2] However, the total number of deputies in the National Assembly can change during each election based on population figures. Deputies serve for five years and are eligible to run for a second term.

Voters elect deputies to the National Assembly in two ways. Venezuela has 23 states in addition to the federal district of Caracas. Each of these districts elects several deputies. Districts with larger populations have more deputies representing them than districts with smaller populations. Voters cast votes for individuals and for a political party. Individuals who receive the most votes are elected. The remaining deputy seats are divided among political parties based on the votes they received. Political parties that receive the most votes are meant to receive more seats. However, government corruption in recent years has resulted in a disproportional distribution of these seats. After the 2020 election, 256 of the 277 seats were controlled by Maduro's allies.[3]

The judicial branch is Venezuela's court system. It includes the Supreme Tribunal, which is the highest court in the land. The Supreme Tribunal has 32 justices, who are elected by the

> Between 1811 and 1999, Venezuela had 27 different constitutions.[4]

National Assembly. Justices are allowed to serve for a single 12-year term. The judicial system makes sure that laws and policies do not conflict with the constitution.

The electoral branch includes the National Electoral Council. The National Assembly selects the five members of the National Electoral Council. These members serve for seven-year terms and are responsible for overseeing and organizing government elections on the federal, state, and local levels.

The citizens' branch is the fifth branch of the Venezuelan government. It includes three positions: the office of the prosecutor general, the defender of the people, and the office of the comptroller general. The three members of this branch are selected by the National Assembly and serve for seven-year terms. The citizens' branch is responsible for investigating the other branches and making sure that government officials are not corrupt.

## POLITICAL PARTIES

Historically, the dominant political parties in Venezuela were the Democratic Action party and the Social Christian Party. They remained the major political parties until 1998, when Chávez was elected president. He was supported by his political party, the Movement of the Fifth Republic. In 2007, Chávez merged this party with several smaller parties that he was also aligned with. This combination became the United Socialist Party of Venezuela (PSUV). Many people criticized the PSUV. Some worried that there would be too many unique viewpoints in the party to create a united front. Others said the united party carried too much power.

President Nicolás Maduro delivered an address before the Supreme Tribunal in January 2022.

In 2019, protesters gathered in Caracas and demanded Maduro's resignation.

In 2022, the PSUV remained in power. However, both Chávez and Maduro experienced heavy opposition while in office. One major opposition party is the Popular Will party. Juan Guaidó helped establish this party in 2009. The party declares that it will "build a more secure, united and prosperous country where everyone will be entitled to all rights."[5] Oppositional parties, including the Popular Will party, have banded together to create the Unitary Platform. The Unitary Platform hopes to reinstate fair elections in Venezuela.

## THE CHÁVEZ PRESIDENCY

The 1999 constitution was written mostly by pro-Chávez members of government. During the 2000 elections, those who shared Chávez's beliefs won 122 of 131 available legislative seats.[6] Since the National Assembly is in charge of electing members to other branches of government, Chávez had nearly total control over all aspects of Venezuelan government.

By 2002, Chávez's approval ratings had fallen. On April 11, thousands of people marched in the streets of Caracas demanding his resignation. As a result of the protest, a coup ousted Chávez from the presidency for two days. However, Chávez supporters demanded that he be returned to power, and his presidency was restored. Later that year, protests flared again in an attempt to force Chávez to resign or hold new elections. Workers went on strike, including thousands in the petroleum industry. Two months into the strike, Chávez fired approximately 18,000 people working for Petróleos de Venezuela (PDVSA), the government-owned oil company.[7] He replaced the strikers with nonunion workers and foreign employees, effectively controlling PDVSA.

With control of PDVSA, Chávez grew the economy. His approval ratings went up as a result. He implemented social reforms and worked to improve health care and literacy rates in Venezuela. However, the Chávez administration also censored the press. He developed ties with Cuba and Russia. These countries were political rivals of the United States, and US relations with Venezuela suffered as a result. US leaders feared the growing influence of Russia and criticized Chávez's regime. US opposition to Chávez was so strong that it approved of the 2002 coup against him. The US government had known of the coup and did not warn Chávez. This caused political instability and distrust of the US government in Venezuela. Some continue to criticize US involvement in Venezuelan politics.

Chávez was reelected as president in 2006, winning with 63 percent of the vote.[8] He attempted to pass a constitutional referendum that included an amendment that would allow him to run indefinitely. This referendum was narrowly defeated, with 51 percent of voters rejecting it.[9] In 2009, Chávez again tried to get rid of presidential term limits, and this time the referendum passed.

World oil prices declined in 2010. As a result, Venezuela's economy and Chávez's popularity suffered. That year, elections were held for the National Assembly, which then had 165 seats. Chávez's opponents won 65 seats, breaking the two-thirds majority hold that the PSUV had held since 2005.[10]



## CHÁVEZ AND THE UNITED STATES

Chávez had a negative opinion of the US government. He believed that the United States used its wealth to influence smaller nations. For example, in 2001, US president George W. Bush strove to pass the Free Trade Area of the Americas agreement that would reduce trade barriers in the Americas. Chávez thought the plan would benefit wealthy nations and increase poverty in poor countries. Chávez made his opinions about the United States clear and even called Bush the devil in 2006.

# HUGO CHÁVEZ

Hugo Chávez was born on July 28, 1954, in Sabaneta, Venezuela. Chávez and his older brother were raised by their grandmother, who first introduced Chávez to history and politics. As a teen, Chávez was drawn to Bolívar and communist philosopher Karl Marx.

Chávez began his career as a soldier capturing leftist guerillas. But he discovered that his brother was part of this group and sympathized with its cause. In 1982, Chávez and other military officers formed the Bolivarian Revolutionary Movement 200. They staged a coup in 1992 to overthrow the president. Though the coup failed, it helped launch Chávez's political career. He agreed to turn himself in for arrest if he could make a television appearance. In a famous speech, he told viewers that the revolution had failed only for now.

Chávez was released from prison in 1994 and won the presidential election in 1998. He remained president until March 5, 2013, when he died of cancer. Some Venezuelans praise Chávez for helping the working class. However, others criticize him for weakening the country's democracy and causing high inflation rates that still affect the country.

Chávez received 54 percent of the vote in the 2012 presidential election.

Thousands of Chávez's supporters mourned the loss of their leader during his funeral parade in 2013.

In 2011, he went to Cuba for cancer treatment. Despite rising inflation rates and questions about his health, Chávez won another presidential election in 2012. He selected Maduro to serve as his vice president. Between the election and inauguration, Chávez's health declined further. He was unable to attend his own inauguration. He announced that Maduro should be elected president if he was unable to serve. Chávez succumbed to cancer on March 5, 2013.

## DISSOLVING THE NATIONAL ASSEMBLY

The 1999 constitution gave Maduro the authority to dissolve the National Assembly and transfer its responsibilities to the Supreme Tribunal. While facing political pressure in 2017, Maduro declared a state of emergency, which allowed him to dissolve the assembly. The Supreme Tribunal, which was under Maduro's control, took over legislative duties. The Peruvian government was just one of many around the world to criticize Maduro's action, calling it a "flagrant breach of democratic order."[11]

## THE MADURO PRESIDENCY

Because the 1999 constitution says that all public officials must be elected, Chávez's death triggered a presidential election. Maduro won the 2013 election by a narrow margin and was sworn in as president on April 19. The economy suffered during Maduro's presidency. Inflation rates soared while oil prices declined. Maduro's failure to improve the Venezuelan economy led to protests in 2014. At least 28 people were killed.[12] The frustration of the Venezuelan people was evident in the 2016 National Assembly elections. That year, the PSUV lost its majority in the National Assembly for the first time since the party's creation. The National Assembly worked to collect signatures from Venezuelan citizens to trigger a recall vote that would remove Maduro from office.

Threatened by the growing opposition, Maduro dissolved the National Assembly. The PSUV was still in control of the judicial and electoral branches. Though the National Assembly had collected 1.8 million signatures, more than nine times the number needed to trigger a recall vote, the electoral branch refused to cooperate.[13] The electoral branch has also been accused of holding unfair elections. Multiple elections have been delayed, particularly when Maduro's opponents were expected to perform well.

In the following years, protests rocked the nation. The electoral branch continued to make it difficult for citizens to vote for opposing politicians or remove Maduro from office. Maduro was up for reelection in 2018. He had many of his political opponents jailed or disqualified from the race. He also moved the election up from December to May to prevent opponents from having time to organize a winning campaign. Meanwhile, the opposition called for a boycott of the election, believing that it would be rigged and impossible to unseat Maduro. In the election, 68 percent of the votes were cast for Maduro.[14] However, voter turnout was extremely low. The Venezuelan government reported that 46 percent of voters went to the polls for the election, but the opposition believed that the percentage was much lower.[15] Some estimate that as low as 32.3 percent of voters participated.[16]

On January 10, 2019, Maduro was inaugurated for his second term. However, many countries around the world, including the United States, refused to acknowledge Maduro as the Venezuelan

Juan Guaidó declared himself the interim president on January 23, 2019.

president because of the fraudulent election. Shortly afterward, Guaidó declared himself the interim president of Venezuela. As head of the National Assembly, he had the power to do so. The United States and other countries recognized Guaidó as president, but Venezuela remained in political turmoil as the two men fought for control of the country.

# CHAPTER SEVEN

# ECONOMICS

**V**enezuela sits atop the world's largest oil reserves, accounting for nearly 18 percent of known oil sources in the world.[1] Much of the oil is located in the Maracaibo Basin. This region produces approximately 50 percent of the oil that the country exports.[2]

The Venezuelan economy is almost totally reliant on its income from petroleum. The country has been an oil producer since April 15, 1914, when it completed its first oil well on the eastern coast of Maracaibo Basin. Today, oil derricks line the eastern shore of Lake Maracaibo and extend 20 miles (32 km) into the water.[3] More than 15,000 miles (24,140 km) of oil and gas pipelines cross the bottom of the lake.[4]

In 2021, Venezuela produced and exported about 700,000 barrels of oil per day.

The oil industry grew quickly in the 1900s. The Royal Dutch Shell company struck oil in the Maracaibo Basin in 1922. It was able to produce more than 100,000 barrels of oil per day.[5] Annual oil production in Venezuela increased from about one million barrels of oil per year to 137 million barrels in the 1920s.[6] Money poured into the country, and Venezuela's currency—the bolívar—was strong. Soon, oil accounted for 90 percent of the country's exports.[7] By 1929, Venezuela ranked second in the world in oil production, trailing the United States.[8]

In the mid-1900s, the Venezuelan government began to increase its control over the petroleum industry. It passed the Hydrocarbons Law of 1943, which required foreign companies to give 50 percent of their oil profits to the Venezuelan government.[9] Government funds increased dramatically as a result of this law.

Venezuela also became a founding member of the Organization of the Petroleum Exporting Countries (OPEC) in 1960. OPEC includes major oil-producing countries such as Iran, Iraq, and Saudi Arabia. It was formed to ensure that oil prices

Oil from spills washes up on the shores of Lake Maracaibo. In 2016, PDVSA reported that approximately 15 spills occurred every day in Lake Maracaibo.

remained fair and stable. In 1973, OPEC placed an embargo on certain countries as war broke out in the Middle East. Oil prices quadrupled, aiding Venezuela's economy. Venezuela was the richest country in Latin America during the 1970s. At the same time, President Carlos Andrés Pérez nationalized the Venezuelan oil industry, creating Petróleos de Venezuela (PDVSA). This further bolstered the country's wealth.

Venezuela's economy grew increasingly dependent on oil. When global oil prices fell in the

Analysts estimate that the Venezuelan government mismanaged approximately $100 billion in oil-related funds between 1972 and 1977.[10]

**Fishers face constant exposure to oil pollution in Lake Maracaibo, which also affects fish populations.**

1980s, Venezuela's economy suffered. Inflation rates soared, and the country's debt ballooned. Additionally, Venezuela's economic reliance on oil led to social divisions and corruption in the government. Government administrations mismanaged oil funds. Wealth became concentrated in the upper class, while many others lived in poverty.

Venezuela's government stability and economic stability remain linked today. While Chávez was president, he was able to reduce poverty levels for some time because of strong oil prices. But oil prices dropped in 2014 when Maduro was president, sending the economy into freefall and adding to his unpopularity. Today, petroleum accounts for approximately 99 percent of Venezuela's export earnings.[11] The country's oil dependence can also be seen in its gross domestic product (GDP). About 25 percent of Venezuela's GDP comes from oil.[12]

## CURRENCY AND INFLATION

Venezuela's official currency is the bolívar, which has been in use since 1879. However, the currency has changed forms several times to control inflation rates. For example, the bolívar fuerte was created in 2008. Inflation had made the previous bolívar nearly worthless. One bolívar fuerte was equal to 1,000 old bolívars.

In 2018, the Venezuelan government released a cryptocurrency called the petro. The petro's worth is tied to the country's oil reserves. Maduro created the new currency to stabilize the economy. However, the petro did not reduce the country's inflation rates or lower prices.

Because inflation has weakened the bolívar, much of Venezuela uses US dollars. In 2021, more than 60 percent of payments in Venezuela were made using US dollars or through digital platforms such as PayPal.[13] That year, one million bolívars was equal to about 25 US cents.[14] Venezuela did not have enough printed money for people to purchase groceries.

> In 2019, Venezuela's inflation reached 10 million percent.[16]

In January 2022, Venezuela had the highest inflation rate in the world.[15] However, oil prices were increasing, and the economy showed signs of improvement. The government released a new bolívar. A single bill in the new version of the bolívar was equal to one million old bolívars. Additionally, the Maduro government worked to phase out the use of US dollars and increase the circulation of the new bolívar.

Venezuelan coal miners often have to work in dangerous conditions with little pay.

# OTHER NATURAL RESOURCES

In addition to petroleum, Venezuela has other natural resources. It has the second-largest store of natural gas in the Americas, trailing the United States.[17] However, much of its natural gas is used to boost its petroleum industry.

The country also has iron ore, bauxite, gold, diamonds, and other minerals. In 2022, Venezuela made plans to increase its iron ore production. The country is capable of producing 7.6 million short tons (6.9 million metric tons) of iron ore per year.[18] Bauxite was discovered in the Guiana

Highlands in 1974. This rock contains minerals that are used to produce aluminum. The Guiana Highlands also have diamonds and gold.

While oil and natural gas account for most of Venezuela's energy sources, the country also has renewable energy, such as hydropower. The Guri Dam hydroelectric power plant on the Caroní River is one of the largest hydroelectric plants in the world. The plant was completed in 1986. Hydropower supplied more than 68 percent of the country's energy needs in 2020.[19] Venezuela has large rivers and heavy rainfall that make this form of renewable energy effective. However, the effectiveness of hydropower in Venezuela has declined in recent years due to climate change. Drought has lowered water levels in the Caroní River. In addition, the government lacks the funds for maintenance and repairs to make sure hydroelectric plants run smoothly.



## AGRICULTURE AND OTHER INDUSTRIES

Venezuela has fertile land and a tropical climate that supports farming. Agriculture was once a major part of the country's income, but the industry declined in the 1970s due to a growing emphasis on oil. Venezuela began relying on agricultural imports from other countries. Today, Venezuela produces only 30 percent of its food supply.[20]

Though agriculture makes up only 5 percent of the country's GDP, it is still an important industry. Approximately 14 percent of Venezuela's workforce is employed in the agricultural industry. In addition, about 20 percent of the land in Venezuela is used for agriculture.[21]

Venezuela grows crops such as sugarcane, rice, corn, and sorghum. The tropical climate allows farmers to grow fruits including plantains and oranges. Venezuela also produces livestock such as cows and chickens.

Manufacturing is another major industry in Venezuela, accounting for about 15 percent of the country's GDP.[22] Many of the manufactured products are tied to oil. It has many petrochemical plants that produce goods such as plastics, fertilizers, and pesticides. Other factories manufacture items including fabrics and beverages.

Venezuela has a developed transportation system that helps export products and move products internally. Approximately 22,400 miles (36,050 km) of paved roads run through the country.[23] Buses connect most towns. Airports provide access to more isolated areas. Boats carry goods along the Caribbean coast and through riverways. A few railways connect iron and steel mining areas in the Guiana Highlands to market areas in other parts of the country. Pipelines carry oil and gas.

In 2020, the service industry accounted for three-quarters of the jobs in Venezuela.[24] The service industry includes jobs in areas such as banking, real estate, government, hotels and restaurants, and tourism. Venezuela has huge potential as a tourist destination with outstanding natural beauty in its national parks. In 2008, the tourism industry reached $1 billion per year.[25] But due to political instability and high crime rates, tourism in Venezuela has declined since 2013. Many countries, including the United States, do not recommend travel to Venezuela. Despite safety issues and high costs, Maduro tried to grow Venezuela's tourism industry by investing in state-owned hotels. Renovations to the government-owned Hotel Humboldt were completed in 2018. However, many are critical of the restoration and see the hotel as a symbol of the social divide between Venezuela's wealthy and those living in poverty.

# VENEZUELA TODAY

Today, Venezuela faces many issues that stem from the country's economic crisis and governmental dictatorship. The contested 2018 elections plunged Venezuela into further political uncertainty, as both Maduro and Guaidó claimed the presidency. Guaidó received widespread international support, though Russia and China backed Maduro. Despite the support overseas, Guaidó did not have much authority within Venezuela. Maduro remained in the presidential palace, and the military stayed under his control.

In response to the presidential crisis, the United States imposed economic sanctions on Venezuela to

Juan Guaidó, *left*, met with President Lenín Moreno of Ecuador, *right*, in March 2019. Ecuador was one of many countries that supported Guaidó's presidency.

weaken Maduro's power. In 2019, the United States limited the oil it purchased from Venezuela. Though this further weakened the Venezuelan economy, it did not cause Maduro to step down. In some ways, the sanctions even strengthened Maduro's power. Venezuela experienced hyperinflation in 2019, with an inflation rate over 9,000 percent.[1] Many people in Venezuela were unable to afford the rising prices and became increasingly dependent on government aid. Maduro was able to finance his government by increasing oil production and mining gold in the country.



Meanwhile, Venezuelan citizens were frustrated at the lack of change in their country. Guaidó had popular support in February 2019, but by July 2020 his approval ratings had declined from 61 percent to 25 percent.[2] It has been difficult for the opposition to organize under Maduro's tightening dictatorship. More than six million people, many of whom oppose Maduro, have fled the country during his presidency.[3]

On December 6, 2020, Venezuela held elections for the National Assembly. Guaidó had been president of the assembly. As with the 2018 presidential election, Guaidó and the opposition called for a boycott of the election. This time, just 31 percent of Venezuelans voted.[4] Maduro's party won,

A line of Venezuelan asylum seekers carry their belongings across the Táchira River to enter Colombia.

and the National Assembly returned to Maduro's control. The National Assembly had been the last branch of government to be controlled by the opposition.

## HUMANITARIAN CRISES

The Venezuelan refugee crisis is one of the most severe in the world. Many refugees have fled to other Latin American countries in South America or in the Caribbean. While these nearby countries are working to assist the refugees, many lack the resources to accommodate the hundreds of thousands of Venezuelans seeking asylum. In addition, many Venezuelans lack the necessary documentation to live and work in the surrounding countries. They must enter other countries without authorization and may not be guaranteed human rights. Many of the refugees flee Venezuela on foot, which puts them at risk for being captured and sold for human trafficking.

Refugees have left Venezuela for many reasons. Some do not feel safe in their home country because of their political beliefs. High inflation, extreme poverty, and violent crime are other major factors. More than 94 percent of Venezuelans live in poverty.[5] Rising costs have made food unaffordable to many people. In addition, the government has taken over farms and limited their exports, which has reduced profitability. Many farmers do not have enough money to ensure that their crops and livestock stay healthy. Agricultural output has declined. Amid food shortages, Venezuelans are forced to turn to the government for meals. Maduro has refused humanitarian relief from other countries for the situation.

Hunger and poverty affect many Venezuelan children. A 2017 report found that 11.4 percent of children younger than five were moderately or severely malnourished.[6] Three-quarters of Venezuelan adults in 2016 reported losing an average of 19 pounds (8.6 kg) that year due to the lack of food in the country.[7] Food shortages and lack of medicine contributed to the country's infant mortality rate, which rose 30 percent between 2016 and 2017.[8] The prevalence of diseases

**More than 1.8 million Venezuelan refugees have settled in Colombia since Maduro became president in 2013.[9]**

such as malaria and Zika has also increased in the country since 2017.

Venezuela has one of the highest crime rates in the world. This is worsened by the country's economic and political instability. Human trafficking, weapon smuggling, and illegal drug distribution are highly profitable crimes. The economic crisis has also caused people to join gangs and mafias. The rise of these criminal groups has made Venezuela even more dangerous in recent years.

## COVID-19 IN VENEZUELA

Many of the humanitarian issues in Venezuela were worsened by the COVID-19 pandemic. The country reported its first COVID-19 cases on March 13, 2020. By July 2022, the country had more than 526,000 confirmed cases.[10] However, the actual number of cases was

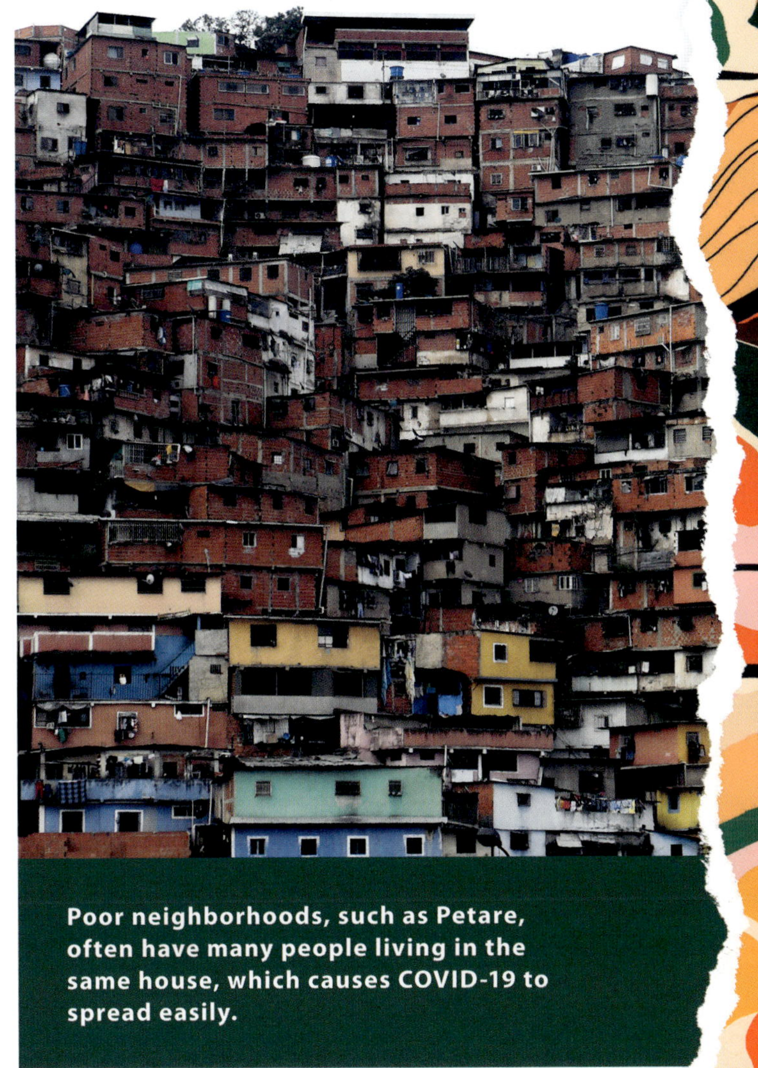

Poor neighborhoods, such as Petare, often have many people living in the same house, which causes COVID-19 to spread easily.

likely much higher, as Venezuela lacked adequate testing and was slow to report data. Some experts estimate that the true numbers were five to seven times higher than what the government reported.[11] The pandemic highlighted the shortcomings of Venezuela's health-care system. The country lacked the medical equipment and supplies necessary to care for its sick. Some hospitals did not have reliable access to electricity and water. Poverty and malnutrition also affected how well individuals were able to fight off the disease.

Venezuela also had a shortage of doctors. In 2014, there were 66,138 doctors in the country.[12] By August 2019, nearly 50 percent of Venezuelan doctors had left the country.[13] Those who remained earned very little money. Their paychecks were often less than six dollars a month. Because they lacked proper protective equipment, doctors and hospital workers made up about one-third of deaths due to COVID-19 in Venezuela.[14] Some hospital workers were afraid to speak up about the poor conditions, fearing that they would be arrested for criticizing the Venezuelan government.

Maduro did turn to other countries for aid. However, he was selective about which countries and organizations to accept help from. He mainly accepted aid from his political allies, which included Russia, China, and Cuba. Due to staff shortages and the low amount of testing supplies, COVID-19 test sites remained extremely limited in the country. In 2020, Venezuela was able to conduct only 264 tests each week, and there were often long delays for results.[15]

COVID-19 affected the economies of nations around the world. The pandemic caused many Venezuelan refugees to lose their jobs, forcing them to return to their home country. The uncertainty in Venezuela's political future and failure to handle the pandemic added to the country's economic struggles. Some foreign businesses reduced involvement in Venezuela.

## ENVIRONMENTAL ISSUES

Venezuela's environmental organizations receive little support from the government. Maduro even censored environmental data, making it difficult for other governments to know about the environmental challenges Venezuela faces. The oil and mining industries have negatively affected the environment. These industries have expanded in attempts to bring economic stability to the country.

Oil spills and leaks have a significant impact on the environment. Between 2010 and 2016, Venezuela reported more than 46,000 oil spills.[17] In mid-2022, Venezuela had not released new data about oil spills since 2016. The spills affect ocean wildlife and coastal habitats. Mangrove trees along the Caribbean coast have been damaged or killed by oil, which has increased erosion in the area.

Since 2016, more than 568,340 acres (230,000 ha) of forest have been destroyed in Venezuela's rain forests to clear the way for mining.[18] Deforestation has led to other issues, such as flooding. As forests are cleared, there are fewer trees to hold down the soil. Thousands of residents in the state of Mérida have been forced to leave their homes because of mudslides.

Despite the challenges Venezuela faces, the country is still home to more than 29 million people.[19] Some Venezuelans have left the country to seek better opportunities abroad. They can openly speak about the troubles in Venezuela, raising awareness of the humanitarian crisis. For example, many Venezuelan-born MLB players have used their platform to talk about their home country. Miguel Rojas played shortstop for the Miami Marlins in 2022. He volunteered at Raíces Venezolanas, an organization that collects household goods for Venezuelans who have immigrated to the United States. Rojas has spoken about how important Venezuela is to him. "You can never forget about your community, even if they're not in a great place," he said. "In good

Venezuelans celebrated 210 years of independence from Spain in 2021.

and bad, Venezuela is my home country, and I will always come back there and try to help my community."[20]

# ESSENTIAL **FACTS**

# OFFICIAL NAME: BOLIVARIAN REPUBLIC OF VENEZUELA

## GEOGRAPHY

Area: 352,144 square miles
(912,050 sq km)

Highest Elevation: Pico Bolívar at
16,332 feet (4,978 m)

Lowest Elevation: Caribbean Sea at 0 feet
(0 m)

## PEOPLE

Population: 29.8 million (2022 est.)

Most Populous City: Caracas (2.96 million)

Ethnic Groups: Spanish, Italian,
Portuguese, Arab, German, African,
and Indigenous

Religions: Majority Roman Catholicism,
also Protestantism

## GOVERNMENT

Type of Government: Federal
presidential republic

Capital: Caracas

Head of State and Government: President

Legislature: Unicameral, with the
National Assembly

## ECONOMY

Currency: Venezuelan bolívar

Major Industries: Agriculture, machinery
and transport equipment, medicines,
chemicals, iron and steel products, crude
oil and petroleum products

Natural Resources: Petroleum,
natural gas, iron ore, gold, diamonds,
minerals, hydropower

## NATIONAL SYMBOLS

National Anthem: "Gloria al Bravo Pueblo" ("Glory to the Brave People")

National Bird: Venezuelan troupial

National Flower: Easter orchid

# GLOSSARY

**ASYLUM**

Protection given by a country to people who have left their home country as political refugees.

**CAY**

A sand-covered island with coral as a base.

**CENSOR**

To impose values on others by limiting what they may read, write, hear, or see.

**COUP**

An attempt to overthrow government leaders.

**CRYPTOCURRENCY**

A digital form of currency.

**EMBARGO**

A government order that restricts the trade of commodities or goods.

**GROSS DOMESTIC PRODUCT (GDP)**

The monetary value of all final goods and services produced within a nation's geographic borders over a specified period of time.

## INTERIM

For a temporary time period.


## PETROCHEMICAL

A chemical that is obtained from petroleum.


## REFERENDUM

A vote by the general public on a single political question.


## SANCTION

An action taken to punish a country or force it to follow international laws.


## SOCIALIST

Having to do with socialism, a political and economic theory that advocates resources and property being shared equally among members of society.


## SUFFRAGE

The right to vote in a political election.


## TREE LINE

The altitude where trees can no longer grow.

## SELECTED BIBLIOGRAPHY

Minster, Christopher. "The Complete Story of Venezuela's Revolution for Independence." *Thought Co*, 30 May 2019, thoughtco.com. Accessed 9 June 2022.

Schipper, Jan. "Cordillera De Merida Páramo." *One Earth*, 2022, oneearth.org. Accessed 9 June 2022.

"Venezuela's Chavez Era." *Council on Foreign Relations*, 2022, cfr.org. Accessed 9 June 2022.

## FURTHER READINGS

Hand, Carol. *Bringing Back Our Tropical Forests*. Abdo, 2018.

Parks, Peggy J. *Science and Sustainable Wildlife Habitats*. ReferencePoint, 2018.

St Louis, Regis, et al. *Lonely Planet South America*. Lonely Planet, 2022.

## ONLINE RESOURCES

To learn more about Venezuela, please visit **abdobooklinks.com** or scan this QR code. These links are routinely monitored and updated to provide the most current information available.

## MORE INFORMATION

For more information on this subject, contact or visit the following organizations:

**Caracas Museum of Contemporary Art**
F4X2+C56
Cultural de Parque Central
Nivel Lecuna, Avenida Bolivar
Caracas, Venezuela
The Caracas Museum of Contemporary Art houses works by world-famous artists including Pablo Picasso and Claude Monet. The museum opened in 1973 and is one of the most well-known museums in Venezuela.

**Embassy of Venezuela to the United States**
1099 30th St. NW #2
Washington, DC 20007
us.embajadavenezuela.org
The Venezuelan embassy in the United States has information about tourism as well as other information about the country.

# SOURCE NOTES

## CHAPTER 1. A TOUR OF VENEZUELA


1. Ayenat Mersie. "Venezuelan Cocoa Piles Up in New York as Exporters Scramble for Cash." *Reuters*, 7 June 2019, reuters.com. Accessed 6 July 2022.

2. Simon Romero. "In Venezuela, Plantations of Cacao Stir Bitterness." *New York Times*, 28 July 2009, nytimes.com. Accessed 6 July 2022.

3. "Active Pursuits in Caracas." *Frommer's*, 2022, frommers.com. Accessed 2 Aug. 2022.

4. "Explore Diving in Venezuela." *PADI*, 2022, padi.com. Accessed 6 July 2022.

5. Charlie Devereux. "In Venezuela, Public Transport Is a Gondola to a Barrio." *Christian Science Monitor*, 16 Mar. 2010, csmonitor.com. Accessed 6 July 2022.

6. "Explore Diving in Venezuela."

7. "Canaima National Park." *UNESCO*, 2022, whc.unesco.org. Accessed 6 July 2022.

8. "Canaima National Park," *UNESCO*.

9. "Canaima National Park." *National Parks*, 2022, national-parks.org. Accessed 6 July 2022.

10. Kim O'Connell. "Traveler Special Report: Venezuela's Imperiled National Parks." *National Parks Traveler*, 2022, nationalparkstraveler.org. Accessed 6 July 2022.

11. Heather D. Heckel et al. "Venezuela." *Encyclopedia Britannica*, n.d., britannica.com. Accessed 6 July 2022.


## CHAPTER 2. GEOGRAPHY


1. "Venezuela." *CIA World Factbook*, 22 June 2022, cia.gov. Accessed 6 July 2022.

2. Sally Barber. "What Is the Climate Like in Venezuela?" *USA Today*, 24 Mar. 2019, traveltips.usatoday.com. Accessed 6 July 2022.

3. "Natural Hazards in Venezuela: Travel Safety Tips." *World Nomads*, n.d., worldnomads.com. Accessed 6 July 2022.

4. Heather D. Heckel et al. "Venezuela." *Encyclopedia Britannica*, n.d., britannica.com. Accessed 6 July 2022.

5. "Climate – Venezuela." *Climates to Travel*, n.d., climatestotravel.com. Accessed 6 July 2022.

6. "La Tortuga Island." *Tourist Link*, n.d., touristlink.com. Accessed 6 July 2022.

7. Nerio Ramírez et al., "The End of the Eternal Snows: Integrative Mapping of 100 Years of Glacier Retreat in the Venezuelan Andes." *Taylor & Francis Online*, 26 Oct. 2020, tandfonline.com. Accessed 2 Aug. 2022.

8. Kyla Mandel. "Venezuela's Last Glacier Is about to Disappear." *National Geographic*, 26 Nov. 2018, nationalgeographic.com. Accessed 6 July 2022.

9. Heckel et al., "Venezuela."

10. "Lake Maracaibo." *Encyclopedia Britannica*, 17 Feb. 2020, britannica.com. Accessed 6 July 2022.

11. Agnieszka Gautier. "The Maracaibo Beacon." *NASA Earth Data*, 28 Sept. 2016, earthdata.nasa.gov. Accessed 6 July 2022.

12. "Médanos Isthmus: Médanos de Coro National Park (Venezuela)." *LAC Geo*, 21 Oct. 2018, lacgeo.com. Accessed 6 July 2022.

13. Marek Brys. "Orinoco River." *World Atlas*, 9 Aug. 2021, worldatlas.com. Accessed 6 July 2022.

14. Heckel et al., "Venezuela."


## CHAPTER 3. PLANTS AND ANIMALS


1. Amber Pariona. "The World's 17 Megadiverse Countries." *World Atlas*, 5 Feb. 2021, worldatlas.com. Accessed 6 July 2022.

2. "Animals in Venezuela." *AZ Animals*, n.d., a-z-animals.com. Accessed 6 July 2022.

3. Pariona, "The World's 17 Megadiverse Countries."

4. "Troupial." *Dallas World Aquarium*, 2022, dwazoo.com. Accessed 6 July 2022.

5. Pariona, "The World's 17 Megadiverse Countries."

6. "Venezuelan Andes: Cordillera de Mérida (Venezuela)." *LAC Geo*, 11 July 2021, lacgeo.com. Accessed 6 July 2022.

7. "Giant Rosette Plants." *Ecology Center*, 22 June 2022, ecologycenter.us. Accessed 6 July 2022.

8. Julia F. Morton. "Nance." *Purdue University*, n.d., hort.purdue.edu. Accessed 6 July 2022.

9. Jan Schipper. "Llanos." *One Earth*, 2022, oneearth.org. Accessed 6 July 2022.

10. "Green Anaconda." *National Geographic*, 2022, nationalgeographic.com. Accessed 6 July 2022.

11. "Electric Eel." *National Aquarium*, 2022, aqua.org. Accessed 6 July 2022.

12. Ed Yong. "The Truth about Electric Eels Has Long Been Overlooked." *Atlantic*, 10 Sept. 2019, theatlantic.com. Accessed 6 July 2022.

13. Henry Morgan. "Venezuelan Orchids – The Most Complete Guide." *Garden Style*, 2022, thegardenstyle.com. Accessed 6 July 2022.

14. Rebecca Renner. "This Dog-Size Lizard Is Spreading through the Southeastern U.S." *National Geographic*, 18 Nov. 2020, nationalgeographic.com. Accessed 6 July 2022.

15. Jeanfreddy Gutiérrez Torres. "Trafficked Tropical Animals: The Ghost Exports of Venezuela." *Mongabay*, 1 Oct. 2015, news.mongabay.com. Accessed 6 July 2022.

16. Gutiérrez Torres, "Trafficked Tropical Animals."

## CHAPTER 4. HISTORY

1. "Warao and Kariña." *Minority Rights*, 2022, minorityrights.org. Accessed 6 July 2022.

2. "Coro." *Encyclopedia Britannica*, 23 July 2014, britannica.com. Accessed 6 July 2022.

3. Karen Larkins. "Endangered Site: Port City of Coro, Venezuela." *Smithsonian Magazine*, Mar. 2009, smithsonianmag.com. Accessed 6 July 2022.

4. Jason Margolis. "Venezuela Was Once the Richest, Most Stable, Democracy in Latin America. What Happened?" *World*, 7 Feb. 2019, theworld.org. Accessed 6 July 2022.

5. Margolis, "Venezuela Was Once the Richest, Most Stable, Democracy in Latin America."

6. Brian A. Nelson. "Hugo Chávez." *Encyclopedia Britannica*, 1 Mar. 2022, britannica.com. Accessed 6 July 2022.

7. Heather D. Heckel et al. "Venezuela." *Encyclopedia Britannica*, n.d., britannica.com. Accessed 6 July 2022.

## CHAPTER 5. PEOPLE AND CULTURE

1. Kenneth Kimutai too. "Ethnic Groups in Venezuela." *World Atlas*, 18 July 2019, worldatlas.com. Accessed 6 July 2022.

2. "Factbox: Venezuela's Indigenous Groups and Their Struggles." *Reuters*, 9 June 2011, reuters.com. Accessed 6 July 2022.

3. Heather D. Heckel et al. "Venezuela." *Encyclopedia Britannica*, n.d., britannica.com. Accessed 6 July 2022.

4. "Venezuela." *CIA World Factbook*, 22 June 2022, cia.gov. Accessed 6 July 2022.

5. "Venezuela," *CIA World Factbook*.

6. César Augusto Márquez. "Alejandro Carrasquel: The Man Who Opened the Door to Venezuela." *La Vida Baseball*, 11 July 2018, lavidabaseball.com. Accessed 6 July 2022.

7. Chris Brown. "Miguel Cabrera Records His 3,000th Career Hit." *FanSided*, Apr. 2022, motorcitybengals.com. Accessed 6 July 2022.

## CHAPTER 6. POLITICS

1. Brian A. Nelson. "Hugo Chávez." *Encyclopedia Britannica*, 1 Mar. 2022, britannica.com. Accessed 6 July 2022.

2. "Venezuela." *Freedom House*, 2021, freedomhouse.org. Accessed 6 July 2022.

3. "Venezuela Appoints New, Pro-President Electoral Council." *France 24*, 5 May 2021, france24.com. Accessed 6 July 2022.

4. "Venezuela, Constitutions." *Encyclopedia.com*, 2019, encyclopedia.com. Accessed 6 July 2022.

5. Jeff Wallenfeldt. "Juan Guaidó." *Encyclopedia Britannica*, 24 July 2021, britannica.com. Accessed 6 July 2022.

6. Brian A. Nelson. "The Education of Hugo Chávez: Unraveling Venezuela's Revolutionary Path." *VQR*, 2011, vqronline.org. Accessed 6 July 2022.

7. "Venezuela's Chavez Era." *Council on Foreign Relations*, 2022, cfr.org. Accessed 6 July 2022.

8. "Venezuela Profile – Timeline." *BBC*, 25 Feb. 2019, bbc.com. Accessed 6 July 2022.

9. "Venezuela's Chavez Era," *Council on Foreign Relations*.

10. "Venezuela's Chavez Era," *Council on Foreign Relations*.

11. Jonathan Watts. "Venezuela Opposition Allege Coup as Supreme Court Seizes Power." *Guardian*, 30 Mar. 2017, theguardian.com. Accessed 6 July 2022.

12. "Venezuela Profile – Timeline," *BBC*.

13. Heather D. Heckel et al. "Venezuela." *Encyclopedia Britannica*, n.d., britannica.com. Accessed 6 July 2022.

14. Heckel et al., "Venezuela."

15. "Venezuela Election: Maduro Wins Second Term amid Claims of Vote Rigging." *BBC*, 21 May 2018, bbc.com. Accessed 6 July 2022.

16. "Venezuela Election," *BBC*.

## CHAPTER 7. ECONOMICS

1. Samuel Stebbins. "These 15 Countries, as Home to Largest Reserves, Control the World's Oil." *USA Today*, 22 May 2019, usatoday.com. Accessed 6 July 2022.

2. John Staughton. "Why Does Venezuela Have So Much Oil?" *Science ABC*, 9 Feb. 2022, scienceabc.com. Accessed 6 July 2022.

3. "Lake Maracaibo." *Encyclopedia Britannica*, 17 Feb. 2020, britannica.com. Accessed 6 July 2022.

4. Agnieszka Gautier. "The Maracaibo Beacon." *NASA Earth Data*, 28 Sept. 2016, earthdata.nasa.gov. Accessed 6 July 2022.

5. Amelia Cheatham, Diana Roy, and Rocio Cara Labrador. "Venezuela: The Rise and Fall of a Petrostate." *Council on Foreign Relations*, 29 Dec. 2021, cfr.org. Accessed 6 July 2022.

6. Cheatham et al., "Venezuela."

7. Cheatham et al., "Venezuela."

8. Cheatham et al., "Venezuela."

9. Cheatham et al., "Venezuela."

10. Cheatham et al., "Venezuela."

11. "Venezuela Facts and Figures." *OPEC*, 2022, opec.org. Accessed 6 July 2022.

12. Cheatham et al., "Venezuela."

13. "Venezuela Unveils New Currency with 6 Fewer Zeros." *NBC News*, 1 Oct. 2021, nbcnews.com. Accessed 6 July 2022.

14. "Venezuela Unveils New Currency with 6 Fewer Zeros," *NBC News*.

15. "Inflation Rate by Country 2022." *World Population Review*, Jan. 2022, worldpopulationreview.com. Accessed 6 July 2022.

16. Valentina Sanchez. "Venezuela Hyperinflation Hits 10 Million Percent. 'Shock Therapy' May Be Only Chance to Undo the Economic Damage." *CNBC*, 3 Aug. 2019, cnbc.com. Accessed 6 July 2022.

17. "Venezuela." *Robert Strauss Center*, n.d., strausscenter.org. Accessed 6 July 2022.

18. Adriana Carvalho. "Venezuela Restarts HBI Production under New Development Plan." *S&P Global*, 22 Sept. 2021, spglobal.com. Accessed 6 July 2022.

19. Hannah Ritchie and Max Roser. "Venezuela: Energy Country Profile." *Our World in Data*, 2020, ourworldindata.org. Accessed 6 July 2022.

20. "How Deep Is Venezuela's Food Crisis?" *Gro Intelligence*, 30 Jan. 2019, gro-intelligence.com. Accessed 6 July 2022.

21. "Analysis of Agriculture in Venezuela: Production, Consumption, Import, Export and Forecasts (2020–2025)." *Mordor Intelligence*, 2022, mordorintelligence.com. Accessed 6 July 2022.

22. Benjamin Elisha Sawe. "What Are the Biggest Industries in Venezuela?" *World Atlas*, 9 Nov. 2018, worldatlas.com. Accessed 6 July 2022.

23. Heather D. Heckel et al. "Venezuela." *Encyclopedia Britannica*, n.d., britannica.com. Accessed 6 July 2022.

24. Teresa Romero. "Services Sector as Percentage of Total Employment in Venezuela from 2015 to 2020." *Statista*, 30 Mar. 2022, statista.com. Accessed 6 July 2022.

25. Barclay Ballard. "Venezuela's Tourism Industry Tanks as Violence Proliferates." *Business Destinations*, 5 Oct. 2018, businessdestinations.com. Accessed 6 July 2022.

## CHAPTER 8. VENEZUELA TODAY

1. "Venezuela's Inflation Tumbles to 9,586% in 2019: Central Bank." *Reuters*, 4 Feb. 2020, reuters.com. Accessed 6 July 2022.

2. Ciara Nugent. "'Maduro's Grip on the System Is Now Total.' Venezuela's Opposition Faces Uncertain Future after Parliamentary Elections." *Time*, 7 Dec. 2020, time.com. Accessed 6 July 2022.

3. John Otis. "The U.S. Predicted His Downfall but Maduro Strengthens His Grip on Power in Venezuela." *NPR*, 8 Dec. 2021, npr.org. Accessed 6 July 2022.

4. "Venezuela: Maduro and Allies Win National Assembly Poll - Partial Results." *BBC*, 7 Dec. 2020, bbc.com. Accessed 6 July 2022.

5. Monica Weinberg and Julia Braun. "Life in Venezuela, Where 94.5% of the Population Lives below Poverty Line." *Veja*, 1 Nov. 2021, veja.abril.com.br. Accessed 6 July 2022.

6. "Children Face Hunger Crisis in Venezuela as Malnutrition Soars." *Caritas*, 16 May 2017, caritas.org. Accessed 7 July 2022.

7. Mariana Zuñiga and Nick Miroff. "Venezuela's Paradox: People Are Hungry, but Farmers Can't Feed Them." *Washington Post*, 22 May 2017, washingtonpost.com. Accessed 7 July 2022.

8. Zuñiga and Miroff, "Venezuela's Paradox."

9. Kathryn Reid. "Venezuela Crisis: Facts, FAQs, and How to Help." *World Vision*, 12 Jan. 2022, worldvision.org. Accessed 7 July 2022.

10. Hannah Ritchie et al. "Venezuela: Coronavirus Pandemic Country Profile." *Our World in Data*, 7 July 2022, ourworldindata.org. Accessed 7 July 2022.

11. Luke Taylor. "The Venezuelan Health-Care Workers Secretly Collecting COVID Stats." *Nature*, 25 Aug. 2021, nature.com. Accessed 7 July 2022.

12. Gustavo Ocando Alex. "A Doctor or Nurse Might Earn Just $6 a Month in Venezuela." *NPR*, 6 Sept. 2019, npr.org. Accessed 7 July 2022.

13. Ocando Alex, "A Doctor or Nurse Might Earn Just $6 a Month in Venezuela."

14. Moises Rendon. "COVID-19 in Venezuela: How the Pandemic Deepened a Humanitarian Crisis." *CSIS*, 23 Sept. 2020, csis.org. Accessed 7 July 2022.

15. Rendon, "COVID-19 in Venezuela."

16. "Venezuela." *Reuters*, 7 July 2022, graphics.reuters.com. Accessed 7 July 2022.

17. Ryan C. Berg. "The Role of the Oil Sector in Venezuela's Environmental Degradation and Economic Rebuilding." *CSIS*, 12 Oct. 2021, csis.org. Accessed 7 July 2022.

18. Kenneth Roth. "Venezuela: Events of 2021." *Human Rights Watch*, 2022, hrw.org. Accessed 7 July 2022.

19. "Venezuela." *CIA World Factbook*, 22 June 2022, cia.gov. Accessed 7 July 2022.

20. Christina De Nicola. "How Venezuela Shaped López, Rojas." *MLB*, 27 Sept. 2021, mlb.com. Accessed 7 July 2022.

## CYNTHIA KENNEDY HENZEL

Cynthia Kennedy Henzel has a bachelor of science in social studies education and a master of science in geography. She has worked as a teacher-educator in many countries. Currently, she writes fiction and nonfiction books and develops education materials for social studies, history, science, and ELL students. She has written more than 100 books and over 150 stories for young people.